Steam Memories On Shed: 1950's - 1960

No. 91 DERBYSHIRE ENGIN

D BEECROFT, D DALTON & K PIRT

Copyright Book Law Publications 2016
ISBN 978-1-909625-59-4

INTRODUCTION

This album has been created to illustrate some of the engine sheds, and their locomotives, which existed in Derbyshire during the British Railways era when steam was still the chosen motive power. Not all of the depots extant during that time are presented; Dinting for instance, and Hayfield to name but a couple of the sub-sheds. In no particular order we do include Buxton, Hasland, Barrow Hill, Staveley GC, Derby, Westhouses, Langwith Junction, Rowsley, Friargate, Staveley Works; also included is Burton-Upon-Trent which, as you may tell yourself, was in Staffordshire. However, we have put it in amongst the Derbyshire sheds for three reasons (1) it was coded 17B under Derby (2) the county boundary was just a stones throw away-ish! (3) If the shed was still in existence it would have a Derby DE post-code! Enjoy.

David Allen, Newstead Abbey, 2016

(Cover) See page 48.

(title page) Derby had been turning out diesel shunting locomotives for years and of course they were responsible for the two pioneering main line diesel locomotives which appeared either side of Nationalisation – 10000 and 10001. Then they built the BR Sulzer Type 2s and Type 4s but in between the bouts of dieselisation, they also built some steam locomotives such as this Standard Class 5 No.73077 which was put into traffic on 13th May 1955 at Eastfield. Standing alongside No.4 shed with other ex-works engines, the 4-6-0 will be undergoing a series of test runs to make sure all is good prior to its trip north to its new home. People often quote the life-span of the BR Standard 9Fs as the epitome of waste but this particular engine was operational for just nine years and many of the Scotland based members of the class managed just eight years service! Still, in 1955 when 73077 was new, the future looked rosy. Derby's final batch of Class 5 construction – Caprotti equipped 73145 to 73154 – was put into traffic in the summer of 1957 and they too went to the Scottish Region.
Don Beecroft.

Printed and bound by The Amadeus Press, Cleckheaton, West Yorkshire
First published in the United Kingdom by Book Law Publications, 382 Carlton Hill, Nottingham, NG4 1JA

BUXTON

The former L&NWR shed at Buxton in April 1960. Opened in 1892, this depot replaced a smaller establishment sited nearer the station on the west side of the main line to Stockport. Of period design, the six-road building was a typical northlight roofed shed with raised vents over each road. Brick walls and a slated roof completed the construction. In this view, the shed is in remarkable condition – those few missing pieces of wood on the ventilator troughs were no problem – considering the somewhat exposed location and there are even a set of doors on the right hand road although what was original and what has been renewed is unknown. The doors are painted a red-lead colour as are the awnings above the first three roads. The doors were in fact, and most unusually, sliding doors which spanned the 4th, 5th and 6th roads and the 'missing' doors may well have been hidden behind the 'in situ' doors. However, motive power depots and doors did not really get on too well so the fitting of these examples were probably viewed as temporary. In the event, those No.6 road doors survived to the end of steam and closure of the depot (little wonder really because they were never opened as No.6 road inside the shed was not used from about 1930). Note the different sizes of snowploughs in the yard. Such appliances were very important all over the railway system in certain winter conditions but Buxton especially relied on them for survival during certain winters! The Fowler 2-6-4 Class 4 tank, No.42371 was one of Buxton's prized locomotives and was the final one of a batch numbered (4)2365 to (4)2371 received new at 9D during August and September 1929. Two more: (4)2381 and (4)2382 arrived in 1935. The semi-enclosed cabs on these engines were most welcome but the ability of the locomotive to haul whatever was given to them was what really mattered. *Don Beecroft.* 3

There wasn't that much which Sir William Stanier got wrong during his time as C.M.E. of the LMS but one of his first 'dabbles' into LMS locomotive design concerned the construction of ten 2P 0-4-4 push-pull tank engines built at Derby in 1932. The 58-ton engines turned out to be something of a disappointment and those sheds which had an allocation rarely used them, especially in BR days as here at Buxton on 7th September 1958 with, from left to right, Nos.41906, 41905, and 41908, this last one was still allocated to Longsight but they were not making a song and dance about its disappearance somewhere in the Derbyshire hills. Noticeable are the liveries carried thus: 41906 plain black, no lining, new BR crest; 41905 plain black, no lining, old BR emblem; 41908 lined black, with old BR emblem. The trio are stored in the north-east corner of the shed yard near the ash lifting plant. They would not be working again and all three were condemned just over a year later during the week ending Saturday 28th November 1959. Coincidentally all the other class members except No.41900 were withdrawn that same week.

David Dalton.

It is May 1960 and Buxton's own Stanier 2Ps, Nos.41905 and 41906, have been taken out of their storage location and brought onto the shed yard to be made ready for their trip to the scrapyard. Coal is still in both bunkers but the private scrap yards didn't mind a bunker or tender load of coal turning up in their yards but this pair were destined for Crewe and BR Works did not like coal in any part of a locomotive so someone has a job of shifting that lot prior to departure of the pair. Note the wrong facing BR crest adorning 41906's tank side! The route taken by these engines and their 'escort' to Crewe would be via Stockport Edgeley where a reversal was made and the melancholy band set off again.

Don Beecroft.

Once the Buxton pair had been pulled out of the storage road on the depot's eastern boundary, homeless No.41908 was left alone to await an inevitable end; the only question to be asked was when was that going to be? With the benefit of hindsight, we can say that this engine apparently met its end at Gorton works along with sister No.41907, the other member of the Longsight pair which was actually at home. Note that works plates still adorn the tank side, the number plate was still affixed to the smokebox door and the bunker plate is also in situ. The date is May 1960 and the souvenir hunters are still unsure about what to bag. Apologies for those out there who think we may have over indulged with these three images of the Stanier 2P 0-4-4T but it isn't everyday we see hide nor hair of them in this series.

Don Beecroft.

A rather grotty 8F No.48108 makes use of the turntable in July 1966. A newcomer to the shed, this 2-8-0 had transferred from Aintree during the previous May. As to be expected, the Merseyside shed did not bid it farewell with the best of intentions. No.48108 succumbed before the shed closed and was withdrawn in August 1967. On the left of this image is one of the Independent snowploughs which BR invested in during the Sixties, utilising redundant locomotive tenders. Out subject here is DB965228 which would have been a handy piece of kit in these parts. That beast went to the new diesel depot where it could quietly carry on its role in life for many more winters.

Don Beecroft.

We are looking at a class of locomotive which became Buxton's premier workhorse, the former L&NWR G2 class 0-8-0. This is No.49406 buffered up to the stops outside the locker room in May 1960. The G2 is probably awaiting works attention because it was far from finished at 9D although it looks rather jaded. A recent acquisition in the great scheme, the 0-8-0 had come from Speke Junction via a couple of months at Stockport Edgeley. The 'double cab' or tender cab may not have come with the engine, Buxton cherishing these 'far from perfect' but 'better than nothing' appendants attached to these basic tenders. Up here in the High Peak, these tenders were gold. No.49406 was withdrawn in June 1963, the previous winter probably being one too many or was the G2 being worn out? It wasn't an old locomotive but considering its daily grind, nearly forty-two was old enough. Crewe being very efficient in this matters managed to scrap the 7F in one day – 4th October 1963!

Don Beecroft.

As a sort of treat for LNW freight locomotive enthusiasts, we show the other side of a Buxton 0-8-0 in May 1960 but this one is a G2A, No.49348 and it too has a tender cab (No.1182 I think). Now this engine is somewhat older than 49406, about twenty years older and it's seemingly semi-retirement here is in fact yet another Buxton steed awaiting the call to the scrapyard. No.49348 had been withdrawn in the previous November (week ending 14th). Starting life as No.1891 in December 1901 as a 'G' class, it became a 'G1' in December 1920 and then 'G2A' in June 1940. Renumbered 9348 in August 1927, it joined Buxton's allocation from Preston shortly after Nationisation. Cut up at Crewe works 28th April 1961   *Don Beecroft.*

Time for one more and this too is a 'G2A', No.49210 in May 1960. Buxton had sixteen of these 7Fs when British Railways came into being. By 1950 that number was halved but then remained static until 1959. Probably the greatest gathering of 0-8-0 tender engines at Buxton was during WW2 when twenty-one G1s (6) and G2As (15) called this place home. No.49210 was withdrawn in October 1961 and cut up at its birthplace Crewe on 24th November 1961. This view looking south-west across the 'new' turntable pit (actually installed during the yard modernisation circa 1935) reveals another 7F – 49400 – undergoing brake repairs in the yard; remember the month of May in Buxton was positively balmy once the incessant wind had dropped.

Don Beecroft.

On the 4th April 1968, three cold 8Fs wait on the extended shed yard for the inevitable, a month after the closure of Buxton, many relics of the steam age were still in situ – note the water carriers alongside the shed for instance – but others had disappeared, the number and shed plates, along with the tender plates had gone from the locomotives as though a swarm of locusts had descended and then moved on. No.48442 is nearest the camera, the other two were not listed. For the record, No.48442 was one of the wartime Swindon built engines and started life at Old Oak Common in June 1944; it went to the LMS in April 1947 and was allocated to Kirkby-in-Ashfield for the first time. In March 1952 it moved to Mansfield for an eight year stint before returning to K-in-A; Toton was next in February 1961 but it went back to K-in-A that July. Finally in February 1967 9L (Buxton's new and unfamiliar shed code implemented from September 1963 whilst Newton Heath took 9D) beckoned. The relationship was brief and with the closure of the shed the 8F was itself withdrawn.

David Dalton.

Ex-Midland Railway 3F No.43278 had long been on Buxton's strength along with sisters Nos.43268, 43271, 43274, 43282, 43296 and 43387. In this view from May 1960 the 0-6-0 looks far from well, its tender especially appearing in need of some attention! Withdrawn during the previous December – week ending Saturday 19th – it was not quite the last of that batch which entered BR service from LMS ownership at Buxton. No.43268 was withdrawn in June 1961 and was actually the last of them still at Buxton. Meanwhile, No.43271 had moved on to Hellifield and it too was withdrawn December 1959; 43274 remained at 9D but it was taken away in January 1959; 43296 was an early casualty and went in March 1954 still part of the Buxton allocation. Nos.43282 and 43387 both transferred to Warrington Dallam with mixed fortunes, the latter being part of the December 1959 cull whilst the former went on to greater things ducking and weaving the Axe man until October 1962. Our subject here was taken to Derby on an unknown date and cut up at the works there. Note that plates are still attached whilst the vacuum hose has been seconded. *Don Beecroft.*

HASLAND

Hasland shed as seen from a passing train on 4th April 1960. Less than a year beforehand the rumour factory had forecast that Hasland was to close, its allocation transferred to Staveley GC shed; the obvious candidate to receive the 8Fs and six-coupled locomotives would have been Barrow Hill but that establishment too was rumoured to be under threat. However, this period of BR's life – remember the organisation was just over ten years old – was full of turbulence, change, transition, call it what you like, and good old rumour. In the event, the shed was to remain operational until September 1964 but because of the growing diesel fleet, the shrinking steam fleet and the somewhat dire condition of the shed building closure was inevitable. This view shows Stanier 8F No.48559 ready to go off shed on a Monday afternoon, no doubt to take up a nearby colliery working and make its way home to Rugby. The disposal gang look towards the cameraman whilst they seemingly take a break. Behind the mess hut are two shelters, the nearest is to protect the coaling gang who filled the tubs of the 'Lynn' type coaling plant, a concession from BR who decommissioned the original coaling stage which was anything but safe by 1948. The roof of the engine shed had been removed in 1959 as a safety measure rather than a maintenance matter; subsidence from local coal mining had rendered the shed building unsafe with collapse imminent.
David Dalton.

Hasland Sunday 30th August 1964: Just a week before closure, WD No.90529 (in the usual livery of dirty black) stables in one of the stalls off the still functional turntable. How the authorities managed to have total faith in the turntable is to be admired (nowadays such 'irresponsible behaviour' would no doubt generate numerous reprimands) but looking at that wall and its temporary buttresses the shed was somewhat dangerous for all concerned. The WD, it will be noted, was a Eastern region engine which had found its way to Hasland from nearby Barrow Hill 41E; one of the Swindonised' examples, 90529 wears the tall clack valve cover fitted to all the WDs which started their BR careers on the Great Western or Western Region. Alongside the 'Austerity' is Hasland's sole diesel locomotive, a 350 h.p. 0-6-0 diesel-electric shunter which arrived at Hasland brand new from derby on 31st October 1959. Like the 2-8-0, and the rest of the depots charges, the diesel is filthy, a victim of the lack of personnel, and a general malaise coursing through the motive power department staff at this time. D3792 was transferred to Toton on the day of closure – 7th September 1964 – where it found further employment but only for a couple of months before it moved onto Derby on 28th November. It settled down at 16C and was renumbered 08625 under the TOPS scheme but that is another story.

BLP collection.

The relationship between the Stanier 8F and Hasland engine shed was somewhat patchy compared with some other Midland sheds and even in the BR period they were rather shy. During the LMS period three of the class joined the small army of 3F and 4F 0-6-0 tender engines which were the mainstay of the motive power at 18C. That trio comprised Nos.8013 and 8014 in December 1936; they were joined by 8061 during the following April but neither of the three stayed long with the initial pair moving out in September 1938, and No.8061 going in January 1940. All three were called up for war service and with only the latter engine returning for BR service. BR supplied the first 8Fs to Hasland in November 1954 when Nos.48065 and 48095 joined the allocation for a fruitful eight years. From then onwards the Stanier marvels arrived as follows: 48371 in February 1955; 48212 in November 1956; seven in 1957 – 48002, 48116, 48125, 48205, 48359, 48364, and 48547; Nos.48089 and 48527 in January and October 1958 respectively; four in 1959 (48494 in January, 48056 in May, and 48187 and 48284 in November); 48215 and 48447 in January 1960; and finally 48495 in August 1963. Most stayed into the 1960s with 48205 being the last to leave in summer 1964 and making its way to Bolton. This view on Thursday 30th July 1964 reveals three of them in the yard with visiting No.48350 which was a recent acquisition by Kettering but not for long as it went to Derby in September then joined the great exodus to Lancashire for the final days of steam before withdrawal. No.48350 eventually went in September 1967 at Trafford Park.

BLP collection. 15

On the same day that the previous image was captured, this apt scene was captured inside the roundhouse and featured Jinties 47611 and 47543. The wall on this the north side of the building is non-existent except for a few bricks lay in the remains of the structure; scaffolding is acting as a kind of barrier to stop people from falling over the remnants which is somewhat ironic with every pit in the shed open for the unwary. *BLP collection.*

Another visiting 8F simmers inside Hasland roundhouse on the penultimate day of July 1964. Birkenhead's No.48033 has come over to the north Midlands for a train of coal and will overnight here prior to working back to the Wirral via the Hope valley and the lines around south Manchester. This particular 8F was one of the few early examples which didn't do Government service during World War Two, instead it worked for a number of the sheds featured in this album. The walls in this section of the shed are worthy of comment in that at least they stood to the end, albeit with a little help from copious amounts of stout timber.

BLP collection. 17

BURTON UPON TRENT

The use of four-coupled short wheelbase locomotives in and around Burton-Upon-Trent was an everyday occurrence. Most of the industrial concerns in the town – breweries – had their own fleets large and small but the Midland Railway, not forgetting the other two pre-Grouping railways which reached Burton, the GNR and L&NWR, had to construct their own to negotiate the awkward and tight lines built around the town. One of the legacies of BR was the Caledonian railway which also built a class of its own 0-4-0ST and BR, along with the LMS beforehand, used the former Caley tanks to work the lines around Burton. This is No.56020 in store at 17B on 10th February 1952. The saddletank came to Burton during the conflict of WW2, the only one of its class to do so and it remained until November 1952 when it transferred to Bromsgrove in rather strange circumstances which ...! Well that's another story to be related when Bromsgrove engine shed is covered later in this series. In the meantime, the little 0-4-0ST looks perfectly settled in open winter storage with its extra long chimney cover which was obviously specially made. Burton also housed a couple of the L&YR 0-4-0STs, Nos.51217 and 51235 at Nationalisation but the latter moved on to Derby whilst No.51217 stayed until November 1953 when it transferred to Derby but in May 1955 it too was called away to Bromsgrove but managed to escape some four months later. There is plenty to tell about Bromsgrove and its thirst for 0-4-0STs when the time is right!

David Dalton.

18

They liked their Midland 4-4-0s at Burton and when BR came into being the shed had ten of the 2Ps on the books. No.40453, one of the 1890s batch, came after 1948. This is the 2P in the shed yard in April 1959 after a visit to works for some front-end attention. Again, the engine is in winter storage.

Brian Wall.

Redundant, or 'stored' in railway parlance, 0-6-0s outside the 1892 shed during July 1958. Nearest is one of the Rebuilt 2Fs, No.58160, which came from a class which dated from 1875, nearly as old as the first shed. In February 1960 this 2F was resurrected and sent off to Barrow-in-Furness.
Brian Wall.

Burton had seen many 'Jubilees' run past the shed with inter-regional express passenger services for nearly two decades before the first of the class was allocated. When they did come, from 13th November 1957, they came in numbers, unprecedented numbers. In what was the largest mass 'Jubilee' transfer in history, eighteen members of the class were re-allocated from the following sheds: Derby, Leicester, Nottingham and Saltley. We are not going to list them all but No.45648 WEMYSS was one of them and here it is on 18th April 1962 looking rather splendid. Less than a year after this image was recorded, the 6P was condemned on 8th February 1963.

Brian Wall.

No.45712 VICTORY tops up with water before heading off shed on 18th April 1962. In total contrast to the previous image, this rather filthy 'Jubilee' transferred to Burton on 15th January 1962 from Kentish Town where similar external neglect had taken place. It was one of a pair coming to 17B in January and these were followed by more in April; comings and goings remained fairly static but with a few more arrivals the depot's 'Jubilee' allocation in April 1964 was twenty-six examples resident. No.45712 was not amongst that number because one year and six days after its arrival at Burton, the 4-6-0 moved on to nearby Derby where it was to put in about ten months work prior to withdrawal. The others at Burton were worked far and wide by the shed with trips to the seaside at Blackpool and Scarborough amongst the summer duties with excursion work. Typically they worked parcels trains and fitted freights and passenger services on the main line to Bristol and north to Sheffield. However, it was becoming difficult to find suitable work for such a distinguished gathering and ten of the throng were put into open storage in 1964 whilst the rest moved on so that by mid October 1964 17B no longer had any active 6P 4-6-0s.

Brian Wall.

Five of the LMS 'Horwich Moguls' – Nos.42818, 42822, 42824, 42825, 42829 – were modified with Lentz Rotary Cam Poppet valve gear during 1931 in an experiment to see how much coal, if any, could be saved. Initially the savings were negligible but after a few years in service, the engines started to show savings of 5% per annum. However, when balanced against the cost of fitting the gear, it was deemed uneconomical in the long run and, the number of cut-offs available was somewhat limited making them slightly unpopular with some drivers. In BR days, 1953 in fact, a further development of the system was introduced whereby cut-offs were infinitely variable to the point where they were similar to Walschaerts valve gear. The newer development was by Reidinger and this is what the gear looked like in service on 42829 in September 1959. *Brian Wall.*

Derby 2P No.40396 stabled in the 1892 shed on 5th October 1959. The much travelled 4-4-0 had transferred to 17B from Carlisle Upperby in April 1957. Prior to the time at 12A, the Fowler rebuild had been allocated to Rhyl. This image inside the Burton shed shows the lattice girders supporting the three-bay design of the latter type of Midland Railway roundhouse. Each of the twenty-four available stalls inside these round sheds would have different lengths of trackage available – evident here where the 4-4-0 is on one of the shorter stalls and the empty stall in the foreground offers probably ten feet more for the wheelbase of a 4-6-0 perhaps. The twin roundhouses dated from different periods, the older adjacent building coming into use in 1870. The depot closed in September 1966.

24 *Brian Wall.*

With 42829 on the left and 42824 up against the buffers, 42822 and her sisters represent three of the five Reidinger Rotary Cam Poppet Valve equipped 'Crabs' allocated to Burton during most of the BR period and their arrival dates were as follows: 42818 – August 1954 from Saltley; 42822 – August 1954 from Saltley; 42824 – January 1955 from Saltley via Rugby Testing Station where it had spent ten months; 42825 – August 1954 from Saltley; 42829 – August 1954 from Saltley. The date of this image is 18th April 1962, just prior to the withdrawals which took place in a relatively short time frame from May to July 1962 as follows: 42818 – 5th May; 42822 – 2nd June; 42824 – 7th July; 42825 – 30th June; 42829 – 30th June. Of course the presence of so many 'Jubilees' at Burton had some influence as to the general well-being of these 'different Crabs' and the 6Ps could easily handle an traffic previously entrusted to the 'Horwich Moguls'. This lot were going nowhere except their designated scrap yards. *Brian Wall.* 25

This view of Stanier '5' No.44817 at Burton on Wednesday 18th April 1962 also shows 'Jubilee' No.45579 peeping out of the wheel-drop shed. The appliance was installed by the LMS at certain depots where it was difficult to locate indoors because of restrictions. Engines from all over used to visit 17B to use the facility, even those from Derby. In the background is the 1870 shed with its different multi-pitched roof profile. At this time the centre section of the roof had been removed for safety reasons. Ironically when the depot closed to steam, the 1892 shed was demolished to make way for a diesel servicing shed and this ancient pile was left undisturbed!

Brian Wall.

LANGWITH JUNCTION

Now, here is a pair of rarities' or were they? At Langwith Junction they were not and a look at their allocation histories reveals that they went to many other parts of the former LNER territory for various periods of time so they were, it seems, no strangers anywhere! In 1941 under the Edward Thompson regime, the LNER drew up plans to create heavy shunting engines from former Great Central 0-8-0 tender engines, the Q4s. Initially twenty-five were planned but only thirteen emerged from Doncaster works between 1942 and 1945. They were classified Q1 Tanks and weighed in at a healthy 73 tons 13 cwt with their 2,000 gallon tanks (the first four topped the scales at only 69 tons 18 cwt because they had 1,500 gallon capacity tanks). Until 1946 they kept their former Q4 numbers but were thereafter renumbered 9925 to 9937. Langwith Junction shed received new No.6139 (69927) from Doncaster works on Boxing Day 1942 but that was not the first of the class to arrive because pioneer No.5058 (69925) had been transferred from Frodingham on 9th November 1942. Their arrivals were the start of a period of uncertainty which persisted until the last of them was condemned (No.69936 of Frodingham) on 15th September 1959. Meanwhile Langwith became home for six of them at various times in LNER days but these two – No.69928 with 69929 behind – were the only resident Q1s when recorded on film during the afternoon of Sunday 31st March 1957 on the shed spur between the turntable and shearlegs (they were the only Q1s allocated to the shed during BR times). Note the squat narrow pipe, with a removable lid, projecting out of the top of the side tank; this was fitted to No.69928 in January 1953 so that water softening tablets could be dropped into the perforated pipe. Langwith Junction shed had notoriously hard water and this was one of the measures taken to combat that problem. No.69929's pipe, fitted in October 1955 was somewhat shorter but can be seen in this view. The pair moved on to Frodingham on June 1958 and both were condemned just over a year later.   *David Dalton.*

The depot here comprised two buildings, a two-road northlight through shed, and a dead-end three road structure which looked more like a carriage shed with shortened cladding on the walls allowing the lower regions of the resident locomotives to be viewed from outside! The two-road shed was built in 1896 and replaced an earlier structure; both had been built by the cash-strapped Lancashire, Derbyshire & East Coast Railway which was soon to be absorbed by the Great Central. The wooden three-road shed was a former carriage shed apparently salvaged from another site and erected shortly after the GC take-over. The life blood of the shed was the movement of coal, not just local trips to the colliery yards but long distance delivery such as east to Whitemoor and other destinations on the old GER (locomotives from the GE territory were daily visitors to Langwith from pre-Grouping days and that continued right into BR days when diesels from Norwich, March and other East Anglia depots started to appear). To the west the depot's stud would travel out to Manchester and sometimes Merseyside. Langwith's importance was mirrored in the fact that a new diesel depot was built around the corner at Shirebrook to carry on the movement of the mineral on which so much of Britain's fortunes had been won. Langwith closed its doors on 6th February 1966 but the adjacent industrial concern took the site over and even utilised the 1896 shed for many years although it didn't apparently quite make its centenary.

Like all those locomotives allocated to east and north Midlands depots (perhaps the whole country) in BR days No.63902 was looking decidedly tired, dirty and worn out. The date is 31st January 1965, a Sunday, and the contents of the tender of the 2-8-0 do have a positive look about them; perhaps Monday would be a good day after all with all that superb coal and a reliable locomotive. No.63902 was one of the original Class O5s with 5ft 6in. boilers, put into traffic in January 1918. As GCR No.412, the 2-8-0 was rebuilt to O4 standard with a 5ft diameter boiler during the summer of 1922 in order to provide a spare boiler for the other O5s; sister No.413 was similarly treated at the same time. Most of this engine's LNER career was spent at Mexborough shed, and it was one of those specially altered spring gear for working to Whitemoor yard at the southern end of the GN&GE Joint line. No.63902 transferred to Langwith Junction from Doncaster on 25th June 1950. It was to be its final shed but some fifteen years would pass before the call to the scrapyard came in the early summer of 1965. The mechanical coaling plant at Langwith was built courtesy of the LNER.

Brian Wall

J11s formed a decent chunk of the Langwith allocation in the 1950s with a dozen, or so, on the books along with about forty 2-8-0s derived from O4s, a handful of assorted tank engines, and approximately a dozen WD 2-8-0s. Having arrived from Immingham on 10th March 1957 (actually it had come direct from a General overhaul at Gorton so would have been in immaculate condition), No.64314 was resident at Langwith Junction when it was coded 40E and, from July 1958, 41J. This image is dated July 1959, more than two years after that transfer from the coast, and shows the 0-6-0 in the yard on the west side of the two sheds, next to the coaling plant. Not looking as clean as it might, the J11 was due a works visit, if only to get a clean, and that took place during the following September. It was only a Light Intermediate overhaul but it set up No.64314 for another three years of operations at 41J before Gorton called for the final time (it was now aged 60 years and 5 months) in late September 1962. *Brian Wall* 29

Another Langwith Junction J11: No.64333 stables outside the two-road shed on 14th July 1959. This would have been the 0-6-0s fourth residency at Langwith, the first taking place in the mid-1930s, then shortly after the outbreak of war for a ten year stint, then for three weeks in January 1958 prior to a year at Tuxford. The final stay at 41J was from the first day of February 1959 until it was condemned in August 1962. Note that this J11 was equipped with steam heating apparatus but the hose connection had been removed for the summer season as they were prone to damage. One peculiarity about this image is the old BR emblem on the tender; No.64333 had a 'General' at Gorton during the summer of 1958 by which time the new BR crest had been applied for a year or so! It begs the question was this tender – No.6228 – given to 64333 because it had been fitted with a briquette tube feeder (its allocation to Tuxford would have prompted such action as, like Langwith, Tuxford also suffered from very hard water) already when it was with J11 No.64377. No.64377 had a 'General' at roughly the same time in 1958 although it arrived at Gorton after our subject and if Gorton could get away with applying a fresh coat of paint they did, which appears to be the case here whereby the appropriately fitted tender – 6228 – was coupled to 64333 without getting either fresh paint or that new crest. It was No.64333's last visit to shops so would have gone to its doom with the old BR emblem. *Brian Wall.*

41J it states on the shed plate and sure enough that is where we are on this last day of January 1965. Anyone who visited Langwith Junction before its closure in 1966 will remember the industrial premises built right up against the depot's boundary and seen here in this south facing view especially. The buildings belonged to W.H.Davis & Sons who excelled in wagon building and repair, their location in the heart of the coalfield being no mistake even though much of the area around them was rural in nature, being farmland in the main. However, coal mines were everywhere in this part of Derbyshire where the border with Nottinghamshire along with its vast coalfield is just a few miles away. What of our O4 here? No.63877 was one of those rebuilt to Part 8 (27th April 1957) when it was resident at nearby Staveley shed. It came to Langwith Junction on 1st March 1964 – it had been here once before during the winter on 1950/51 when it was an O4/1 – and like many other O4s which came here in the 1960s, it was to make Langwith something of a Mecca for enthusiasts as they came in 1965 and 1966 to view some of the last Robinson engines working on BR.   *Brian Wall.*   31

ROWSLEY

The Rowsley shed which entered BR ownership was a bit of a latecomer in the great scheme and was built to a typical Midland Railway design by the LMS, opening in 1924. It had succeeded a short four-road shed located near the station. The new site was ideal for any future extensions but those never materialised, the optimism of the newly formed LMS, or was it the predecessor Midland, was refreshing anyway. This view of the shed yard on an unknown date in the Fifties shows one of the ex-War Department J94 0-6-0 saddletanks which became synonymous with this depot and the Cromford & High Peak Railway which was supplied with motive power by Rowsley shed. No.68013 transferred from Bidston to Rowsley on 11th August 1956 and it wearing a 17D shedplate here. Rowsley shed became 17C from April 1958 so we can safely point to a date within that time frame. The presence of 'Jinty' No.7459 gives us no clues because she was allocated to Rowsley throughout the 1950s. Seven of the J94s were allocated to Rowsley at one time or another in order to work the C&HPR, sub-shedded at Cromford the full list of those seven is: 68006 arrived 11th August 1956 from Bidston, it transferred to Derby on 4th May 1964; 68012 arrived 1st October 1959 ex Gorton, it returned to Gorton on 29th September 1960 but came back to Rowsley on 27th April 1962, moving to Derby on 2nd May 1964; 68013 ex Bidston 11th August 1956 to Derby 4th May 1964; 68030 also ex Bidston 11th August 1956, and was condemned 2nd April 1962; 68034 ex Bidston 17th August 1957, a latecomer, was condemned 22nd October 1962; 68068 from Gorton 8th July 1962, to Derby 21st May 1964; 68079 also ex Gorton 8th July 1962, to Derby 2nd May 1964. The C&HPR didn't close until 1967 so the J94s serving the line worked from Buxton shed after Rowsley closed. They ended up being highly successful. Normally fitted with round head buffers, note that No.68013 is fitted with oval buffers in order to cope with the sharp curves found on the C&HP; all of the above mentioned J94s were fitted with the oval buffers. And all of them it will be noted, arrived at Rowsley during the summer months. *David Dalton.*

The J94s were brought into replace the worn-out North London six-coupled tanks which had worked the C&HPR for many years. This is No.58850 standing where the J94 had been but we have a date for this image which is 7th September 1958. You would think that the 2F 0-6-0Ts would by now have left Rowsley en route to Derby for scrap perhaps but that was not the case, at least as far as this engine was concerned. When the J94s arrived, the ex-NLR tanks at Rowsley were four in number: 58850, 58856, 58860, and 58862. That had been the case for much of the BR period although at the end of the LMS only three: 27505 (58850), 27515 (58856), 27530 (58862), were resident. Throughout WW2 four of the NLR tanks were maintained by Rowsley thus: 27505, 27515, 27527(58860), 27530. Quite a different story from September 1935 when only two of them – 27515 and 27521 – were employed; a sign of the times when Britain was emerging, indeed so was the world economy, from troubled and difficult financial times. It appears that the 2F tanks did not leave Rowsley that easily and were withdrawn as follows: 58856 November 1957; 58860 May 1957; 58862 March 1956. 58850 finally went in September 1960 once the J94s had settled in and got the hang of their duties it appears? Note the two snow ploughs ready for action in the not too distant future.

David Dalton. 33

Nos.58850 and 58856 in store at the rear of the sand drying house, 31st March 1957. *(below)* Another aspect of the stored NLR pair, at an earlier date, and nearer the shed this time. 58856 had no chimney cover as yet. *both David Dalton.*

For the modellers amongst you, this nice view of the east side of the engine shed reveals some detail of the sand drying house and adjacent buildings. What a terrific 'little' chimney! No.58850 has been thrown into the mix to add scale; the 0-6-0t was working shed pilot duties about then. Oh yes, the date – May 1960 shortly after the completion of the re-roofing of the engine shed.   *Don Beecroft*.

Just in case you thought this section of the album had been devoted to a NLR locomotive special, we present the southern end of the shed in May 1960 with its posh new brickwork on the gables blending in with the original. Fairburn Class 4 tank No.42137 was a visitor from Leicester but the shed had a handful of these useful locomotives on the books. An unknown 9F displays its tender but which one it was could be anyone's guess because Rowsley was then home to four of the class. Within a couple of years that number was to rise to eighteen, albeit not all at the same time, but 17C could boast fourteen 9Fs for working their heavy and long distance freight from the nearby yard. However, although nearly all of the 2-10-0s remained at Rowsley to the very end, four moved on in 1962 and 63. One of the later arrivals was former Crosti No.92022 which came in July 1963 and was amongst the majority sent away when the shed closed on 27th April 1964. Rowsley's time as an engine shed was done and today you would be hard pressed to find any trace of the depot which was demolished shortly after closure.

Don Beecroft.

STAVELEY BARROW HILL & WORKS

Ex-LMS 3F tank No.47630 rests in between bouts of activity as shed pilot at Barrow Hill in May 1960. The 'Jinty' arrived at Barrow Hill in November 1954 from Toton and joined a host of other resident 0-6-0T at the former Midland shed. This view shows much of the shed yard in a quiet period with the ash plant poised ready for the next load of shed spoils. Although now part of the Eastern Region, coded 41E for just over two years, Barrow Hill's locomotive stud at this time was still predominately LMS and nearly half the sixty-odd residents were of Midland origin. Of course, change was in the air but although the diesel population was growing, the remaining and dwindling steam locomotive allocation kept an LMS presence (even the WD 2-8-0s which replaced the Stanier 8Fs came mainly from depots in LMR territory). The shed roof, just discernible in the distance, had been renewed in 1958 and that useful renovation saw the shed through years of diesel use. In 1997 it was sold to Chesterfield Council who then leased the shed and its site to the Barrow Hill Engine Shed Society. The rest, of course, is history. *Don Beecroft.*

Another 0-6-0T in the yard at Barrow Hill: This view shows the use of glass in the wall screen at Barrow Hill, the north and south walls (the side effectively) were clad in corrugated materials as can be see in the following image. The date is 9th November 1960 and former Midland '2441' class No.47221 is eking out the last years of its life on duties here – it arrived at 18D from Cricklewood in July 1956. This was the end of the line for 47221 and in October 1961 the condensing tank was withdrawn.

David Dalton.

Inside the refurbished roundhouse on 15th May 1965 when the remnants of the working steam population was rubbing shoulders with the diesel occupants. The diesel is Clayton Type 1 D8612 one of thirteen allocated to Barrow Hill. Besides the Claytons, English Electric Type 1s and BR Sulzer Type 2s were shedded here. Later came the Type 3s, Type 4s, and the mighty Type 5s as Barrow Hill continued its role of providing the motive power to shift the vast quantities of coal from the local collieries.

Brian Wall.

The two-road shed inside the Staveley works complex in May 1960. This building replaced an older shed and was built to house the Midland and later LMS engines working for the Staveley Company under the Agreement of 1866. As can be seen, the roof is quite unusual in that it was of Dutch barn design, for reasons unknown, and it had a central raised smoke vent of similar profile. Our locomotive subject is No.41769, one of the numerous Johnson 1F 0-6-0T built between 1878 and 1899. No.41769 is one of those which acquired a full cab whereas many kept the original half-cabs. Staveley housed most of the last dozen or so of the operational engines of this class, many of those still sporting the half-cab. No.41769 was a latecomer to the Staveley fold during the summer of 1957; prior to which it had spent much of its life at Upper Bank near Swansea. *Don Beecroft.*

Long-time Staveley resident Johnson 1F No.41708 shows off nicely the half-cab and the temporary measures fitted to the bunker and cab roof to hold the tarpaulin cover/sheet when it was rolled into position to give some protection from the weather. This image is dated May 1960 and shows a clapped-out and by now rather ancient tank locomotive coming towards the end of its illustrious career for these little 0-6-0s were the unsung heroes of the British railway system; their daily toil went unheralded, unrecorded, and for the greater part of their lives unseen. *Don Beecroft.* 41

Another half-cab, No.41804, stables near the shed in the Staveley works precinct. Note the two shunting or barrier wagons – P644 and P596 – for internal works use only. The rolled-up tarpaulin weather sheet is prominent on the cab roof of the 1F. Again this photograph was recorded in May 1960 and the 0-6-0T is wearing a 41E shedplate denoting Staveley Barrow Hill, which was now part of the Eastern Region after boundary changes in February 1958.

Don Beecroft.

STAVELEY GC

Thompson O1 No.63652 stables outside the rebuilt Great Central shed at Staveley in May 1960. During the rebuilding process, the shed was cut down from twelve roads wide to just five, all the smoke vents of which are visible here. Just above the personnel door in the shed wall is the circular brick ornamental housing for the shed clock which was there for all to see; the clock is long gone and ordinary common bricks now fill the void where it sat for fifty-odd years or so. The 2-8-0 was a newcomer to Staveley GC, arriving on 14th February 1960 from March. Its external condition reflects the general attitude of the authorities to steam motive power during this period although lack of manpower at the depots didn't help the cause. This engine was rebuilt from O4/4 No.6371 at the end of 1945, one of Thompson's better designs, No.63652 did two stints at 41H, the second one from 9th June 1963 being its last anywhere for it was condemned a week after Bonfire Night 1963 and then sold to a scrapyard in Beighton the following spring.

Don Beecroft. 43

Many LNER classes had worked from Staveley over the decades since the shed was opened in 1892 but one particular class had evaded the place until 1960 – the Gresley K3. In January 1960 the Eastern Region was desperately trying to diesel-ise the eastern area of the former Great Eastern section and eliminate steam altogether. During the period from 31st January to 24th April they sent thirteen of the 2-6-0s on transfer to Staveley from the depots at Lowestoft, March, Norwich and Stratford. The unlucky thirteen were all placed in outside storage at Staveley until new homes could be found for them where they might get in some useful work. Mexborough took half a dozen whilst Langwith Junction had three, and Colwick and Lincoln had a couple each. it took nearly two years to get rid of them but the deed was completed on 3rd June 1962 when Nos.61826 and 61973 were packed off to Colwick, job done! However, in the meantime two of those sent to Mexborough had been transferred to Millhouses and when that establishment closed the pair were sent to Staveley on 10th September 1961. Thwarted, the Staveley top brass had no option but to condemned the pair – 61959 and 61989 – just a couple of weeks after the 'Colwick two' had departed. This is No.61908 which arrived from March on 14th February 1960. Note the new 41H shed plate which leads one to assume that Staveley had ideas about using the K3s in the first instance and may well have done during the early days. The 2-6-0 has no indication of being in store so may well have been put into traffic initially. *Don Beecroft.*

A view of the depot from the south-east in May 1960; this reveals the areas where sections of the original shed were removed permanently. Much of the area became used for open storage in the 50s and 60s, the D11 'Director' No.62661 GERARD POWYS DEWHURST being a typical annual winter resident. The 4-4-0 transferred to Staveley on 7th June 1959 from Darnall, joining No.62663 PRINCE ALBERT which had arrived fourteen months earlier. The latter engine was condemned in the month when the photographer captured these images and, like No.62661, had been engaged on the Sheffield-Chesterfield-Nottingham local passenger services when actually employed. Both engines also worked an evening train to Leicester. Of course our subject doesn't appear capable of working anything anymore and it was condemned on 18th November 1960 and sent to Doncaster for scrapping. Note the name and number plates still attached but a 41H shedplate was absent. The pathway running at right angles across the shed yard behind the 'Director' basically marked the demarkation between those engines stored and those working, at least on the nearest three tracks at that period. That situation was about to change. The two filled-in pits between the photographer and the engines shows the extent of the shed building before demolition and alteration in 1951. *Don Beecroft.* 45

So, we've met the K3s and the D11s which were conveniently dumped here so that they did not clutter-up somebody else's backyard! Now its time to meet the K2s – Nos.61728 and 61747 – a pair of Darnall 2-6-0s which were resident at Staveley in May 1960 after winter storage. Both engines were transferred to 41A in the summer of 1955 and that proved to be their last move after glorious careers spanning 47 years in the case of 61728 and 44 years for 61747. Of course No.61728 had been a K1 until rebuilt during a works visit to Doncaster (28th December 1935 to 8th February 1936). However, loyalty counted for nothing on BR and in December 1960 both of these locomotives were sent to Doncaster for scrapping, 61747 on Monday 5th and 61728 on Tuesday 6th. Returning to the image, and in the background we can see the remaining amenity/office section of the original shed. Note also how the shed roads have been shortened probably too keep heavy weights clear of the area.   *Don Beecroft.*

On an earlier date in March 1959 two 'Directors' are stored for the winter. No.62666 ZEEBRUGGE and 62665 MONS. They were both allocated to Sheffield Darnall and had spent the winter months here as no work could be found for them at 41A. Note both are properly prepared for their hibernation. No.62665 was condemned just weeks after this scene was recorded whilst sister 62666 worked, survived might be a better description of its existence, until December 1960. The eagle-eyed will have noticed that the fairly new wall of the truncated shed has a rather obvious crack developing from that joint at the bottom of the ridge – subsidence, big time! It came with the territory, so-to-speak; Hasland not too far away suffered too as we have already seen. This area of Derbyshire was rife for such damage because of the coal mines. At its height Staveley GC shed looked after the traffic requirements of more than a dozen local mines and the price of doing so is plain to see.

Don Beecroft.

Of course it wasn't all storage and gloom at Staveley. There was plenty of work to employ the depot's freight locomotive stud and typical of them (not the dirt; although yes it was rather widespread here and apparently contagious!) was O4/8 No.63884 which even had a shunters pole on its front plate ready for the next trip to a colliery to collect another load of coal. Some of the coal from the surrounding pits was tripped down to Annesley yard where it was marshalled into trains which then travelled to Woodford at seemingly express freight speeds in the so-called 'windcutters' hauled by Thompson O1s and then latterly by the 9F 2-10-0s which built up a reputation of speed with those workings. However, back to No.63884 which had been a Staveley engine since December 1951. Built in 1919 for the Ministry of Munitions by the North British Locomotive Co., it was purchased 'for-a-song' by the LNER in 1927 as a 'low mileage, been nowhere asset', perfect for a Company which was feeling the financial pinch and which required such superb locomotives for its heavy mineral traffic. During 1940 (apparently in a week at Gorton but it was wartime and extraordinary feats were being performed everywhere) it was rebuilt to an O4 Part 7, and then during the winter months of 1956-57, it was rebuilt again, this time to Part 8 standard. No.63884 left Staveley on 31st January 1960 bound for Mexborough. Note another resident, J11 No.64384 alongside. *Don Beecroft.*

The fortunes of the Staveley locomotive stud waxed and waned with the seasons, besides what might be happening in the mining industry. In March 1959 O4/8 No.63720 was laid-up with others from 41H after a quiet winter but would soon be back in traffic. It was only two years ago that the O4 was rebuilt to Part 8 standard at Gorton but that upgrading did not guarantee total employment – the gradual loss of freight traffic and the growing diesel fleet saw more and more steam locomotives laid-up, sometimes for ever. As it turned out No.63720 did go back to earning its keep although its time at Staveley was nearly finished. It transferred to Mexborough on 4th December 1960 but nine months later went to Langwith Junction to work out its final years, hauling coal of course until condemned on 5th March 1964. Like many of its ilk resident in this area it was purchased for scrap by one of the Sheffield based yards and disappeared in the great cull of the mid-60s.

Don Beecroft. 49

It is sometimes forgotten that engine sheds such as Staveley – where the glamorous passenger working never existed – often housed a vast assorted allocation over the 73 years when it was operational from June 1892 to June 1965. Some twenty-nine classes of locomotives, besides five sub-classes of O4, served the depot during that time. J11 No.64292 was typical of the long serving freight types found at 41H but with the added bonus of vacuum brakes for passenger train and fitted freight train working. The J11 was often used for excursion traffic in the summer months and it was not unusual for these engines to travel out to Skegness, Bridlington, or even Scarborough – a day at the seaside! This one note is also fitted with steam heating which gave it the opportunity of working the Sheffield-Chesterfield-Nottingham stoppers during the winter months. However, no such niceties on this March day in 1959 and it looks as though the depot's solitary J67 – 68591 – is off on a trip somewhere but it wasn't a works visit nor a transfer as the latter took place during the following October when as the last of the former GER 0-6-0Ts it moved to Langwith Junction. This J11 was no spring chicken and was already in its fifty-eighth year but a General overhaul during the previous November has set it up now until its July 1962 condemnation. To say that these engines were reliable all around useful locomotives would be something of an understatement. Their longevity and numerical superiority into the final decade of steam working says it all.

Don Beecroft.

Besides the former Great Central and LNER standard classes working from this shed, the Great Eastern was represented by a number of six-coupled tanks from classes J66, eight which started to arrive from July 1933; J67, nine which came from October 1945; and J69, five which arrived courtesy of BR. They all came from Stratford and all returned that way once their stints were fulfilled. J69/2 No.68591 transferred to Staveley on 1st June 1958 and here she is on the shed yard at Staveley in March 1959 looking every bit as austere as she was built. The little tank moved on to Langwith Junction in October 1959 but was not required there and was taken back to Stratford where it was condemned in January 1960. *Don Beecroft.* 51

The 350 h.p. 0-6-0 diesel-electric shunters which frequented Staveley shed at weekends were merely out-stationed from Darnall and none were ever allocated. The two examples shown here were not recorded in the photographer's notes nor were they subjects of his camera lens that day, which is a pity. The subject of course was J11 No.64313 which had been here since moving from Woodford on 29th November 1953. It would remain here until condemned on 18th May 1961. Although vacuum fitted, No.64313 did not have the steam heating. Considering their usefulness, the J11 class did not become residents of Staveley until 1935 and then only two of them came from Neepsend. The big migration of the class came during WW2 when eight turned up although three of them had preceded those in March 1939.

Don Beecroft.

Two members of staff take a break at midday on Tuesday 14th July 1959. Being a weekday the yard is fairly quiet, most of Staveley engines being out on the road earning revenue. O4 Part 1 No.63845 is turned, coaled and serviced ready for its next duty. Over the years from their first residency here in 1919, Staveley housed no less that sixty different members of the O4/1 class; add in twenty-three other O4s from the O4/2 to O4/8, and a formidable fleet of these useful 2-8-0s engines will be seen to have served the depot. Of course they were not the only eight-coupled engines of GCR design to have worked from Staveley; between November 1903 and September 1943 nine separate members of Q4 class worked here. Some arrived new from the makers (one of those went to France in May 1917 and didn't return home until June 1919) and No.5086 was condemned here in April 1937 having served its whole life – bar the two years across the Channel – at Staveley. Although a rebuild of a Robinson design, the Thompson O1 still had its origins at Gorton and twenty-eight of those were allocated to Staveley over the period from April 1946 to closure of the shed in June 1965. The roll-call of eight-coupled locomotives housed here was formidable but we are not finished yet because some forty-one WD 2-8-0s came and went from August 1947 to June 1965. Some of these 'Austerities' came for six or seven year stints, others for as many months or even days (No.90001 2nd to 9th December 1951; 90269 21st August 1947 to 27th June 1954). They all added to the variety of the motive power here which over the life of the shed has seen many different types from the solitary Y3 Sentinel No.8161/198 which stayed for one week in December 1929 and the long serving N4 tanks (seven came new in 1891 and 1892) which remained loyal to the depot for forty-seven years or so and going nowhere afterwards except for scrap they were so clapped-out from working colliery trips and banking!

Brian Wall. 53

Staveley shed 16th May 1965 just weeks away from closure and O1 No.63786 appears to be in dire straits. And so it was. As can be seen the 2-8-0 had lost a set of coupled wheels and if a getaway to some other depot was to be completed in the next couple of weeks the wheel set would have to be refitted. However, all is not what it seems because the O1 was already condemned, an event which took place on 27th September 1964 when 63786 was not even at home. Wherever it was on that fateful day, it was taken back to Staveley and languished there over the winter of 1964/65, complete with number and shed plates but without those wheels. In November it as sold to a local (Killamarsh) scrap yard and by all intents should have been residing there by New Year. But that as can be seen was not the case. Axles are made from steel which is amongst the most valuable of the ferrous metals and those wheels were worth a few bob too; throw in the coupling and connecting rods and we a talking a few quid in 1960s prices. The scrapyard probably wouldn't take it without said missing bits and so a prolonged period of storage at 41H was on the cards. A compromise price was obviously negotiated with BR and T.W.Ward because the 2-6-0 eventually departed 41H. Does anyone know more about the saga of 63786?

Brian Wall.

C13 No.67419 was one of six of this class serving Staveley at various times over the period from 1st December 1928 to 28th October 1956. They were not all there at the same time and the most which ever gathered here together was two to work the local passenger services to Sheffield. Indeed from 16th May 1939 to 9th December 1951, the shed had none of them on the books, 4-4-0 tender engines of ex-GNR classes D2, D3 and ex-GC D9 having replaced them during the war years and then worked alongside them too on the local passenger duties before and afterwards. N7s Nos.69637 and 69643 arrived from Stratford on 15th July 1951 to take up work on the local passenger services but they both departed on 9th December that same year having apparently done very little work at 38D. No.67419 was one of the pair (67410 was the other) which restored the standing of the former GC engines on the local passenger services. They both arrived at Staveley from Gorton on 9th December 1951 just as the 0-6-2Ts departed back to Stratford. Note the changeover was nicely choreographed, on paper, but I wonder what happened in reality. As can be seen, our subject is in store in that area of the yard where such events took place. The date is 2nd October 1955 and sister 67410 is long gone having been condemned 23rd March 1953. That particular C13 was the first of the class to come here on that December day in 1928 and in all it completed three separate residencies. No.67419 was to complete another year here at 38D before being condemned but it is unknown if she ever worked again. Note the work is still ongoing in the yard with the former shed roads nearer to camera requiring in-fill now that the rails have been removed. The rear of the shed building shows off the staggered finish of the back wall with three of the inner roads running through a shortened section of the shed.

Keith Pirt.

J66 No.68383 stands inside the rebuilt shed on Sunday 2nd October 1955. Transferred from Cambridge on 26th July 1953, this 0-6-0T was condemned 17th October 1955 and was the last of eight of the J66 types serving Staveley. Of the eight, six of them were condemned at 38D – as the shed was then coded (1948 to July 1958 when it became 41H). Keith Pirt photographed the engine again, this time it was outside the shed on one of the roads located on the west side of the building; it was in the company of and coupled to another 0-6-0T, J67 No.68589 bound for Stratford, and oblivion. *Keith Pirt.*

WESTHOUSES

8F No.48214 looks reasonably turned-out at Westhouses in March 1966. A resident here since April 1965, the 2-8-0 was to stay to the very end of steam on 3rd October 1966. It was then transferred to Colwick but in less than a month it was sent to Patricroft where another years work was eked out of the end of steam period. It is debatable if the 8F ever went to Colwick in October 1966 and more than likely it remained at Westhouses awaiting a more positive move to Lancashire. Prior to its time at 16G, No.48214 had been working in the Midlands since entering traffic in September 1942 at Leicester. Nearby Kirkby-in-Ashfield became home from June 1943 until February 1961 when Toton called. K-in-A got it back five months later until November 1963 when Derby required its services; eight months later it was transferred Nottingham who gave it up to Westhouses. The engine could be described as a general run-around for the whole of the area; it certainly looks that way on paper.   *Don Beecroft.*

(previous pages) Westhouses depot as seen from the main line in 1966 before steam was evicted and the diesels took over the place with a vengeance. The six-road building was of typical Midland Railway design of 1890s vintage. The manual coaling stage is still in business – just – and the place is pretty much as it was seventy-odd years beforehand, only the motive power having changed. In this view Stanier 8Fs rub shoulders with BR Standard 9Fs whilst an earlier era is represented by an abandoned and probably withdrawn 4F nearest the camera. Brush Type 4s are the only diesels apparent but that was to change after steam left and English Electric Type 1s and BR Sulzer Type 2s joined the throng especially on Sundays. The reason for this depot's existence is located less than half a mile away in the right background: coal mining, everywhere. From this vantage point in 1966 you could look towards the horizon in the east and glimpse a working colliery, turn left or right and continue turning until you return to your initial stance and virtually every segment of the compass would have revealed a mine or the waste tip of a former mine. Names to conjure with in this local area were; Blackwell 'A', Blackwell 'B', New Hucknall, South Normanton, Brookhill, Bentinck, Langton, Pinxton, Alfreton, Tibshelf, Wingfield Manor, Shirland, etc. etc. The list was seemingly and wonderfully endless with millions of tons of coal being won every year to initially keep hundreds of locomotives busy along with thousands of their crews, fitters, signalmen, platelayers, shunters. Again, a seemingly endless list! Those of us old enough to have been train spotting in steam days probably thought these industries would last forever. They were so embedded in the landscape, the mindset, and every day life that we perhaps took them for granted but everything goes around in a circle, especially human activity and that which we thought would last forever suddenly appeared vulnerable to change and the last sixty years have seen massive change especially here in the East Midlands. The coal industry has gone, its passing hardly noticed by the general public but sorely missed by those involved. The transport industry which supported the coal industry has changed drastically to the point whereby only a fraction of those employed in 1960 are with the railways now. What of this scene here nowadays? You wouldn't know that any of this ever existed. And if you could be bothered to scan the horizon to look for a coal mine you would find the winters here long and hard sometimes.

Keith Pirt.

(opposite) Stranger in town? Most certainly! Caprotti 5 No.44743 graces the shed yard in March 1965 after working in from Speke Junction. What working brought the '5' here and what route it took is unknown but I'm sure the authorities at Westhouses would be glad to see the back of it once it had departed. Ironically this engine would have worked past the shed many times on the main line for it had spent time at Holbeck in its early life but then it went to Bristol, then Derby, Bank Hall, Southport and then back to Liverpool from where it was condemned in January 1966. Anyone who worked these seemingly complicated engines thought they were superb and up to the challenge.

Don Beecroft.

DERBY

The outside turntable at Derby Midland shed, with its numerous radiating stalls, allowed photographers to record more locomotives on film than a conventional straight shed yard might do; as was the case on Saturday 18th January 1958 when Rowsley's 4P Compound No.40931 was resting for the weekend. This was to be the 4-4-0s last year in traffic and in September, after a transfer to Lancaster, it was condemned. *David Dalton.*

Ex-works Compounds share the shed yard at Derby on 31st January 1954. It looks like General overhauls have been the order of the day and No.41086 looks resplendent in the lined black livery. Mechanically at least, the former LMS Derby-built 4-4-0 should be okay for another four years when withdrawal takes place. We do not have the number for the other engine but its tender certainly looks splendid. No.41086 was allocated to Llandudno Junction shed at this time but it would move wet to Holyhead for a couple of years before a transfer to Derby in the summer of 1957 brought it nearer to the works that cared for it; that same works also scrapped these elegant engines. However, although No.41086 was condemned at Derby in May 1958, it was towed away to Crewe to be cut up at the works there.

David Dalton.

The ten former Midland Railway Deeley 0-4-0 0F side tanks of 1907 vintage were, by BR days, mainly congregated around sheds in Derbyshire but two of them – 41530 and 41537 – were long term residents of Gloucester Barnwood shed, used on the docks branch created by the Midland Railway to serve their docks at Gloucester. Occasionally one of them would have to visit main works at Derby, and during its absence the Operating Authorities would send a substitute engine. No.41530 had been withdrawn in May 1957 so No.41537 was 'left holding the fort' so to speak although sister No.41535 had been transferred to Barnwood as a permanent replacement. Meanwhile, No.41537 was required at works in the summer of 1957 and in this undated view inside the roundhouse shed at 17A, the diminutive four-coupled tank is undergoing a few trials and adjustments before its journey back to Gloucester. Whilst in the shops the opportunity as taken to apply the new BR crest and for that to be done a coat of paint was offered to the side tank whereas the rest of the engine merely got a clean. The new crest has helped us to pin down the date to that period in the summer of 1957 when the new crest was introduced, to the time in early 1958 when its application was curtailed after objections by the College of Heralds. The crest we are looking at is in fact one of the wrong facing examples which BR put on the right side of tenders and side tanks so that the lion and wheel would face forwards. On the left side the lion and wheel face forwards too but that is perfectly acceptable in heraldry but a right facing lion is not. BR of course were somewhat miffed at the attitude of the College but if they were to use the crest they had to abide by the rules. Hundreds of the expensive transfers had been made and BR were determined to use them up and had done so by about April 1958 when the new batch of correct left-facing lions were applied to locomotives attending works thereafter. Look out for these particular crests and remember the old adage - left is right, and right is

wrong!

David Dalton.

Replenishing their tenders, resident Ivatt Class 4 No.43010 and ex-works Stanier 8F No.48158 from Holbeck take advantage of the mechanical facilities at Derby on 5th August 1955. The 8F was one of Holbeck's allocation and had spent the back end of July in shops having a front end problem sorted out; the lick of paint around the smokebox and saddle have made the locomotive look even dirtier. This image shows much of the reality of steam locomotive servicing with piles of ash and clinker strewn around areas where it shouldn't be. The ground is made up from a mixture of coal dust and fine ash with the running rails slowly being swallowed. The coal chutes from the overhead bunkers are somewhat worn-out by this date, already nearly twenty years old and not a day had passed in that time when coal had not rushed through the chutes into waiting tenders (a rough calculation of twenty years continuous use once a day would see the number 7,300 appear when in actuality it was multiplied many times with up to a hundred locomotives a day bring attended to; no wonder things got worn out. Oh yes, let's not forget that a minimum of four tons of coal would be discharged each time!). Recreating scenes such as this in model form is quite difficult in order to make it look authentic but they certainly existed.

Don Beecroft.

An undated view across London Road junction in the period when steam was still getting overhauls and new 350 h.p. 0-6-0DE shunters were being turned out with zebra stripes – its probably 1960. The south-west wall of No.4 engine shed is on the left with those new ex-works diesels alongside. Then we have a group of ex-works steam locomotives. The solitary building standing amongst the lines of engines is the weigh house. The next bunch of motive power is a mixture of ex-works on running-in turns, and visiting locomotives. The main line to Trent, Nottingham and London, skirts the stabling lines; beyond are carriage sidings soon to become part of the Research centre.   *Steve Lacey BLP Coll.*

Derby roundhouse on 15th August 1965 with diesels muscling-in on the few places left for steam. Known as shed No.4, this building comprised two adjacent roundhouses of square plan and we are in the shed next to the outside turntable where three openings were available for access in BR days. This shed dated from 1890 and we see it here in the last years of its life because in March 1967 it was closed. Demolition took place two years later to provide space for further diesel servicing facilities. Resident in the shed on this summer Sunday were a couple of diesel-hydraulic shunters, an English Electric Type 3 (a foreign visitor), a Stanier Class 5, and this diminutive four-coupled Kitson-built 0F saddletank of 1932, No.47000, which had done the rounds of the Derbyshire sheds: Burton, Rowsley, Westhouses, and now it was at the parent shed, 17A. However, it had been to Gloucester too with No.1537 in the 1930s. Less than a year away from withdrawal, the little tank is looking its age and the jobs which it was designed to tackle were disappearing (somewhat ironically the four-coupled diesels which had been purchased by BR to replace these engines were also under threat and most of them followed steam to the scrapyard).

David Dalton.

Eastern Region locomotives were no strangers to Derby shed and the fact that Derbyshire was home to both ER and LMR sheds saw plenty of inter-regional 'mingling' although it was rare for a LM shed to use a visiting ER locomotive on a LMR working, and vice-versa. Basically they worked in from their parent region, serviced, perhaps stabled, then worked back; it was very much as it had been prior to Nationalisation. However, conventions are there to be changed or broken and shortly after BR came into being, the BR workshops started to take in certain locomotives which would otherwise never cast a shadow over their doorways. Derby works really went to town and in the thirty-one months starting 1st May 1950 until December 1952 they managed to conduct major overhauls to 159 Class J39 0-6-0 tender engines. Ardsley's No.64806 was photographed at Derby on 28th October 1951 waiting to enter works for rectification after spending a week at 17A running-in. The 0-6-0 had been in shops from 31st August to 22nd October 1951 receiving a Heavy Intermediate overhaul (note that only 'spot' painting was carried out, the full repaint was reserved for 'Generals' only), and obviously something had manifested itself during that week in the care of the running shed. The following fortnight saw No.64806 receive a Non-Classified repair before it returned to Yorkshire. The reason for Derby handling so many of these ER engines was lack of workshop space at Doncaster, Gorton, and Stratford. The event was unparalleled in BR history and perhaps only the Western Region WD 2-8-0 attendance's at Crewe comes anywhere near.

David Dalton.

As a loose follow-on to the last caption, we continue the theme thus: The Stanier 8Fs which were amongst the many classes maintained at Derby for years and therefore seen in numbers at the adjacent engine shed. However, on Sunday 14th March 1965 No.48344 appears every bit an ex-works locomotive but look at those numerals! Of course, the answer was simple enough, the overhaul - a Heavy General - had not been carried out at Derby, not with those size numbers. The 8F was ex-Darlington on Thursday 25th February 1965 after a couple of months residence in County Durham. Derby had finished carrying out overhauls to steam locomotives by this time, Horwich was winding down and Crewe was bulging at the seams doing everything. BR decided to send LM based steam locomotives to either Darlington, or Cowlairs in Glasgow. Being former LNER establishments, both workshops applied those distinctive large numerals (St Rollox was another works that used the large numbers) and so it came to pass. Quite a few dozen 8Fs passed through Darlington shops during the period when they carried out the work, along with a few oddities such as 'Jinty' No.47482 and others. Cowlairs tended to handle the Stanier 5s from Lancashire sheds (they were used to handling the Scottish Region based examples for years) but they too worked on the 8Fs when Darlington closed. So, what was this Trafford Park based engine doing here on this chilly day in 1965? Unsure, I can only surmise that it had worked in from Manchester, or it was en route from Darlington to 9E via Derby where it called in for a check over by LM-based fitters? Whatever the reason, the overhaul was enough to keep the 2-8-0 operational until it moved from 9E to 9F in March 1968; after a month at Heaton Mersey No.48344 was condemned. Derby (Midland) station can be seen in the background and the photographer is standing on the main line to Nottingham, London, and everywhere via Trent.   *David Dalton.* 69

8F No.48618 stables on the shed yard at Derby in May 1956 after attention at the works; it looks as though a 'General' has been administered? Toton based at this time – October 1944 to July 1958 – the 2-8-0 was one of the Southern Railway-built wartime examples which emerged from Ashford works in September 1943 and was allocated initially to Holbeck. The Mk.2 all-welded tender is from the 10327 series and was possibly No.10345 although that fact requires confirmation. The 8F transferred to one of the sheds under review in this album in July 1958 when it went to Barrow Hill. Five years later the magnetic pull of Lancashire saw it move to Newton Heath in May 1963, followed by Fleetwood in the following March. To consolidate its credentials of being amongst the last of BR steam, No.48618 transferred to Lostock Hall in June 1965 but alas did not quite make it to the very end being withdrawn in September 1967.

Don Beecroft.

The low winter afternoon sun of Saturday 8th November 1958 bathes the flanks of 'Britannia' No.70004 WILLIAM SHAKESPEARE as it runs over from the shed, in the background, to the station to take up a working to Manchester (Central). A handful of these Pacifics worked from sheds on the Midland lines during this period. No.70004 was allocated to Trafford Park after transferring from Kentish Town during the previous July. 'The Bard' was to remain at 9E until the end of 1960 when Willesden called and most of the LMR 'Brits' were based on the Western Lines. However, back to 1958 and Nos.70014 IRON DUKE and 70015 APOLLO followed the same path except Newton Heath was the recipient of that pair in December 1960 rather than 1A. No.70017 ARROW, 70021 MORNING STAR and 70042 LORD ROBERTS copied 70004, and then Nos.70031 BYRON, 70032 TENNYSON and 70033 CHARLES DICKENS joined the 9E flock in May and February 1960 and remained at the Manchester shed for the rest of that year. Trafford Park had never had it so good but typically it was a case of too much too late. The diesels were coming and very quickly the BR Sulzer Type 4s had taken over the expresses to St Pancras although 'Scots' and 'Jubilees' had initially replaced the Pacifics.   *David Dalton.*

On Monday 11th January 1954 Colwick based J6 No.64183 attends the coaling stage at the former Great Northern Railway engine shed at Derby Friargate, or Slack Lane to perhaps be more geographically correct. As manual coaling stages go, this edifice was something of 'a luxury' for all concerned. The coalmen loading the coal tubs worked under cover, and the enginemen could water their steed beneath the cover of the somewhat elaborate canopy; a water tank topped the brick-built stage. The four-road engine shed which was now coming towards the end of its operational life, is just discernible in the murk beyond. A classic twin hipped-roof period design, the shed was opened in 1876 as part of the GN's drive westwards from Nottingham. Once beyond Derby however, and away from the collieries which were the lifeblood of the GN in Derbyshire, the line to Stafford lost its importance and became something of a backwater. Such was the reason for the early demise of this establishment which although used as a signing-on point from 1955 onwards for a few years, the shed was hardly used until sold to a local company who refurbished the rather dilapidated roof and turned the building into a store. Still being used in 1997, it may well be standing today! *David Dalton.*